FARM ANIMALS

CHICKENS

Ann Larkin Hansen
ABDO Publishing Company

visit us at
www.abdopub.com

Published by Abdo Publishing Company 4940 Viking Drive, Edina, Minnesota 55435.
Copyright © 1998 by Abdo Consulting Group, Inc. International copyrights reserved in all countries. No part of this book may be reproduced in any form without written permission from the publisher.

Printed in the United States.

Cover Photo credits: Peter Arnold, Inc.
Interior Photo credits: Peter Arnold, Inc.

Edited by Lori Kinstad Pupeza

Library of Congress Cataloging-in-Publication Data

Hansen, Ann Larkin.
    Chickens / Ann Larkin Hansen.
    p. cm. -- (Farm Animals)
    Includes index.
    Summary: Describes the physical characteristics, habits, uses, and needs of this farm animal that was brought to North America by the first settlers.
    ISBN 1-56239-602-1
    1. Chickens--Juvenile literature. [1. Chickens.] I. Title. II. Series: Hansen, Ann Larkin. Farm Animals.
    SF487.5.H36   1998
    636.2--dc20   95-52345
                                                      CIP
                                                          AC

About the Author

Ann Larkin Hansen has a degree in history from the University of St. Thomas in St. Paul, Minnesota. She currently lives with her husband and three boys on a farm in northern Wisconsin, where they raise beef cattle, chickens, and assorted other animals.

Contents

Chickens: Jungle Birds

Chickens decorate farms all over the world. They scratch, cluck, and flap the days away. Farmers keep them for eggs and meat. Chickens also eat bugs, make manure for the garden, and are loads of fun just to watch.

Chickens are all descended from jungle birds. Jungle birds are a kind of Gallus bird that still wander through Burma and Malaysia. Today's chickens don't look much like their ancestors! They are much bigger, more colorful, and lay many more eggs.

Opposite page:
Chickens come from
birds of the jungle.

Easy, Fun, and Useful

Chickens have always been popular with farmers. They are simple to care for and do not take much space. They are also easy to carry when traveling. They spread to China, Europe, and Africa more than 2,000 years ago. The first settlers brought them to North America.

In the nineteenth century, farmers began improving chickens by **selective breeding**. They wanted bigger birds that would lay more eggs. Some farmers wanted chickens that didn't mind heat, and others wanted chickens that could stand cold winters.

Selective breeding has created four types of chickens. **Layers** are small, but lay many eggs each year. Meat chickens grow very rapidly to large sizes. **Dual-purpose** chickens lay a good number of eggs, and are medium sized. They are also the easiest to raise. Bantams are miniature chickens kept mostly for pets and showing.

Chickens are easy to care for.

Breeds

Today there are more than 100 different **breeds** of chickens. The Leghorn is the most common laying type, but Anconas, Hamburghs, Minorcas, and Welsummers also lay up to 350 eggs each year. Jersey Giants and Light Brahmas were early meat types, but today a cross between a Plymouth Rock and a Cornish is most popular, growing to 12 pounds (5.4 kg) or more in just two months.

There are more **dual-purpose** breeds than any other type. Many were developed in America, such as the Plymouth Rock, New Hampshire, and Rhode Island Red. The Buff Orpington can handle cold winters, and Aracaunas lay blue eggs.

Bantam breeds are usually small versions of bigger types, such as the Bantam New Hampshire. Their eggs are smaller, but just as good.

A Plymouth Rock chicken.

What They're Like

Chickens like to live in **flocks** of 20 or so **hens** and one **rooster**. During the day they eat bugs and plants, take dust baths, and scratch in the dirt. At night they go home to their **coop**. They sleep on **roosts**, or long poles hung above the floor.

Hens lay three to seven eggs each week. Eggs are white, brown, or even blue depending on the **breed** of chicken. Usually, the eggs are laid in a nest in the coop. But sometimes hens lay eggs in the barns, or old sheds, or the woods. Then the farmer has to go looking for the eggs!

A rooster.

Fuss and Feathers

Chickens fuss and cluck a lot. They do not like to be held, but come running for food. Only **roosters** crow, often at dawn. They also crow whenever they feel like it, and will fight anything that threatens the **hens**–even people!

Hens make clucking and squawking noises. Every **flock** has a **pecking order**, from the boss hen to the lowliest new teenaged chick.

All chickens are covered with feathers that keep them warm and dry. Feathers come in all different colors. Some chickens have them on their feet. Others have feathers that stick straight up from their heads, or out from their cheeks. A state fair is a good place to look at all the different kinds of chickens.

Once each year, chickens shed old feathers and grow new ones. This is called molting, and can take one to three months. **Hens** do not lay eggs when they molt.

Chickens pecking and clucking.

Combs and Wattles, Feet and Gizzards

The red growth on a chicken's head is called a **comb**. Below the beak are the **wattles**. These help chickens shed heat, since they do not sweat.

Chickens also do not chew, since they have no teeth. Instead, they eat tiny rocks, or **grit**, which goes into the **gizzard**. The muscles of the gizzard use the grit to grind food fine enough to eat.

A chicken also has a crop. A crop is a bag in their neck to store food, just as a chipmunk will store food in its cheeks.

A chicken has three long front toes and one back toe on its foot. **Roosters** also have **spurs** on their legs, which they use for fighting. The toes grip the **roost** tightly at night, so the chicken doesn't fall. Their toes are also perfect for scratching up food.

This rooster has a large comb on its head and a big wattle below its beak.

Senses and Abilities

Like all birds, chickens have very sharp eyes. Their eyes can work together or look in two different directions at the same time.

They hear very well. Their ears are little holes in the sides of their heads, and are covered by feathers. Chickens will learn to recognize the voice of their owner.

They can smell and taste, but their ideas of what is good is very different from humans! They eat almost anything.

Although chickens have hollow bones like other birds, they are not good flyers. Only the bantams fly well enough to **roost** in trees.

Chickens have very good eyesight.

Care

Many wild animals like to eat chickens, especially foxes. Chickens must have safe **coops** that can be closed at night to protect them. A coop must also be dry and not too hot or cold.

In the coop are **roosts**, nests, a feeder, a waterer, and feeders for **grit** and crushed shell. The **hens** need the calcium in oyster shells to make strong eggs.

Some farmers keep chickens in movable coops, which are shifted each day to fresh grass. Coops must be cleaned regularly to keep out lice and other **parasites**.

Opposite page:
Chickens in a barnyard.

Food and Water

Chickens are not fussy eaters. They love table scraps, bugs, and grass. They also should have a special feed that includes salt, minerals, and vitamins. This feed must have a high protein level. The protein comes from fish or bone meal. The rest is made of ground grain, such as corn, oats, or wheat. Chicken feed is sold at farm feed stores.

Chickens need a lot of water. Special waterers are used to keep the chickens from dirtying the water with feed or feet. The water should be cool and changed every day.

Opposite page: A chick eating out of a dish.

Health

Chickens are very healthy birds. They do not usually get sick or have worms. Small **flocks** do not need **vaccinations**. On very large chicken farms, where there may be thousands of birds, farmers do vaccinate. They do not want to take any chances with **coccidiosis**, or other chicken diseases that will kill the whole flock.

Chickens do get external **parasites**, such as lice, fleas, mites, and ticks. Farmers dust **roosts** with parasite-killing sprays to control these pests.

Opposite page: A barred rock hen.

Chicks

Sometimes in the spring a **hen** will get a funny look in her eye. She will refuse to leave her nest, and squawk if anyone comes too near. She has gone **broody**.

A broody hen sits on her eggs for 21 days, leaving only to eat and drink quickly. She turns the eggs each day, and keeps them warm.

After three weeks, the baby chicks peck their way out. At first they are wet, but in an hour they are dry and fluffy. The hen will take very good care of them. She finds food, and tucks them under her wings at night. She will attack anything that might be a threat.

Opposite page: Chicks hatching from eggs.

Hatching Eggs

Today most eggs are not hatched by **broody hens**. They are hatched in **incubators**, which are special heated boxes. When the chicks are dry, they may be packed in cardboard boxes and mailed to their new owners. Since chicks don't need food or water for the first few days of life, this is safe.

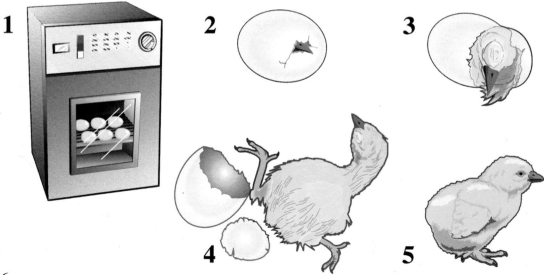

The new owners put the chicks in a **brooder**, an enclosed pen with a heat lamp. They must be kept very warm, and have special chick food. Their beaks must be dipped in water when they arrive, to teach them to drink.

Newborn chicks under warm lights.

Index